Eat Healthy Foods!

Published in the United States of America by Cherry Lake Publishing
Ann Arbor, Michigan
www.cherrylakepublishing.com

Reading Adviser: Marla Conn MS, Ed., Literacy specialist, Read-Ability, Inc.
Book Design: Jennifer Wahi
Illustrator: Jeff Bane

Library of Congress Cataloging-in-Publication Data

Names: Marsico, Katie, 1980- author. | Bane, Jeff, 1957- illustrator. Title: Eat healthy
foods! / by Katie Marsico; illustrated by Jeff Bane. Description: Ann Arbor, Michigan:
Cherry Lake Publishing, [2019] | Series: My healthy habits | Audience: Grade K to 3.
| Includes bibliographical references and index. Identifiers: LCCN 2018034526 |
ISBN 9781534142787 (hardcover) | ISBN 9781534139343 (pbk.) |
ISBN 9781534140547 (pdf) | ISBN 9781534141742 (hosted ebook) Subjects: LCSH:
Nutrition--Juvenile literature. | Health--Juvenile literature. Classification: LCC TX355
.M375 2019 | DDC 613.2--dc23LC record available at https://lccn.loc.gov/2018034526

Printed in the United States of America
Corporate Graphics

table of contents

Healthy Habits: Diet. 4

Glossary 24

Index 24

About the author: Katie Marsico is the author of more than 200 reference books for children and young adults. She lives with her husband and six children near Chicago, Illinois.

About the illustrator: Jeff Bane and his two business partners own a studio along the American River in Folsom, California, home of the 1849 Gold Rush. When Jeff's not sketching or illustrating for clients, he's either swimming or kayaking in the river to relax.

How many colors are in your fruit cup?

Variety is part of healthy eating!

We want a healthy body.
That's why we use good **hygiene**.

It's also why we eat healthy foods.
They form a balanced **diet**.

Foods are divided into groups. Each food group gives our body something it needs.

Some foods help fight off **diseases**.

What's your favorite food?

Fruits and vegetables are two food groups. Both are good for our heart and kidneys.

Grains are a food group, too.

Rice, bread, and pasta are grains.

Grains give us energy.

What do you like to do when you have lots of energy?

Protein foods are also a group.

Meat, **poultry**, and seafood have protein. So do beans, peas, eggs, nuts, and seeds.

Protein is good for our blood and bones.

We also need dairy foods.

Milk, yogurt, and cheese are a few.

Dairy is important to teeth and bones.

We even need a little oil in our diet. It gives us **vitamins**.

Yet not all oils are healthy.

Foods made with vegetable, fish, and nut oils are healthy.

How much of each food group should you eat?

Ask your doctor!

A lot depends on your age and your body.

Try new foods often!

Color your plate with different fruits and vegetables.

Find tasty ways to be healthy!

What are some of your healthy habits?

glossary

diet (DYE-uht) the food that is regularly eaten to stay strong and healthy

diseases (dih-ZEEZ-uhz) sicknesses or illnesses

hygiene (HYE-jeen) keeping yourself clean or other actions that support good health

poultry (POLE-tree) chickens or other farm birds kept for their eggs or meat

protein (PROH-teen) a nutrient found in certain foods that is important for our body's cells to develop and work properly

variety (vuh-RYE-uh-tee) having many different forms or types

vitamins (VYE-tuh-muhnz) nutrients made by plants and animals (which our body needs to grow and work properly)

index

balanced, 6
body, 6, 8, 20
bones, 14, 16

color, 4, 22

groups, 8, 10, 12, 14, 20

healthy, 4, 6, 22